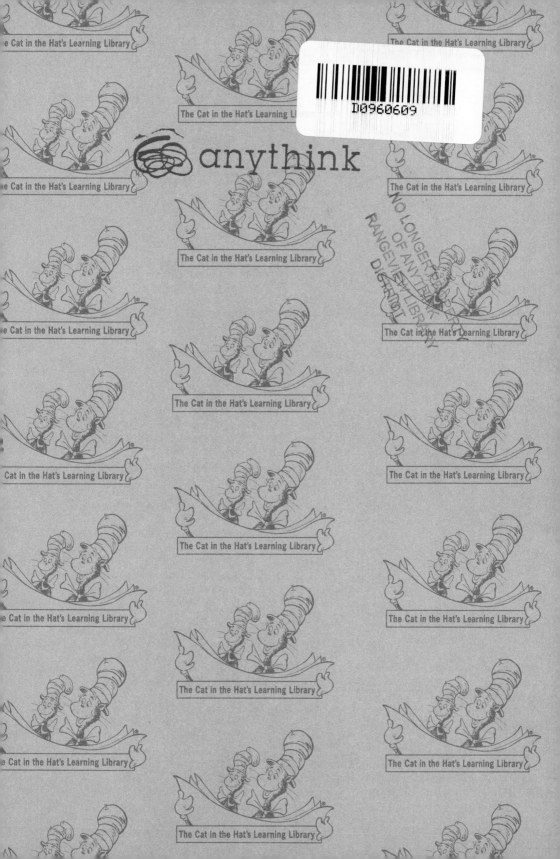

anythink

There's No Place Like Space!

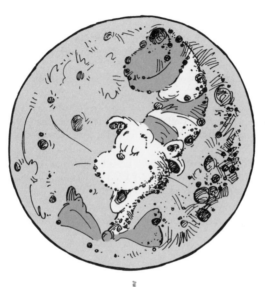

To John with love—T.R.

The editors would like to thank
BARBARA KIEFER, Ph.D.,
Charlotte S. Huck Professor of Children's Literature,
The Ohio State University,
AMIE GALLAGHER, Astronomy Educator,
The Hayden Planetarium at the American Museum of Natural History, and
LANCE TANKERSLEY, Omnisphere Director,
The Coca-Cola Space Science Center,
for their assistance in the preparation of this book.

Visit us on the Web!
Seussville.com
randomhousekids.com

Educators and librarians, for a variety of teaching tools, visit us at RHTeachersLibrarians.com

Library of Congress Cataloging-in-Publication Data
Rabe, Tish.
There's no place like space! / by Tish Rabe.
  p. cm. — (The Cat in the Hat's learning library)
Summary: Dr. Seuss's Cat in the Hat introduces Sally and Dick to the planets, stars, and moons in our
universe.
ISBN 978-0-679-89115-4 (trade) — ISBN 978-0-679-99115-1 (lib. bdg.)
1. Astronomy—Juvenile literature. [1. Astronomy.] I. Title. II. Series.
QB46.R28 1999 520—dc21 97-52315

Printed in the United States of America   60 59
Revised Edition

There's No Place Like Space!

by Tish Rabe

illustrated by Aristides Ruiz

The Cat in the Hat's Learning Library®

Random House 🏠 New York

I'm the Cat in the Hat,
and we're off to have fun.
We'll visit the planets,
the stars, and the sun!

There is no place like space.

I will prove it to you.

Your mother will

not mind at all if I do.

Jump in! Here we go!
We will fly up so high
we can dance on the moon
and play games in the sky.

We will swing past the stars,
and in case you have missed 'em,
you'll soon see...

the planets
in our solar system!

There are eight of these planets
that circle the sun,
and soon you'll be able
to name every one.

Mercury's

close to the sun's burning light.

It is hot in the daytime...

but freezing at night.

On Venus the weather
is always the same—
hot, dry, and windy,
with no chance of rain.

TODAY's WEATHER ON VENUS: REALLY, REALLY HOT! NEARLY 900° FAHRENHEIT! WINDY and DRY

Can you guess the next planet?
Well, here is a clue:
It is my home and home
to Thing One and Thing Two.

You have been living on it
each day since your birth.
It is third from the sun—
it is **our** planet...

...Earth!
It spins all the time,
round and round like a top.
It turns once every day
and it never will stop.

HOME
SWEET
HOME

This question had Thing One and
Thing Two in a tizzy:

If the Earth's always spinning,
why don't we feel dizzy?

We don't feel the Earth
as it spins on its way
'cause we're spinning right with it
right now every day.

Next, here is Mars.
It's the color of rust.
We sneeze here because
it is covered with dust.

Travel to Jupiter
and you will find
it is bigger than all
other planets combined.

Saturn has rings.
It's so light—
who would think?

It could float in an ocean
and not even sink!

A planet can have
satellites that surround it.
Uranus has lots of these
objects around it.

There are colors in space.

I will show some to you.

Neptune, planet eight,

is a beautiful blue.

We have seen all the planets.

Now here is a trick

to remember their names

and remember them quick.

Say:

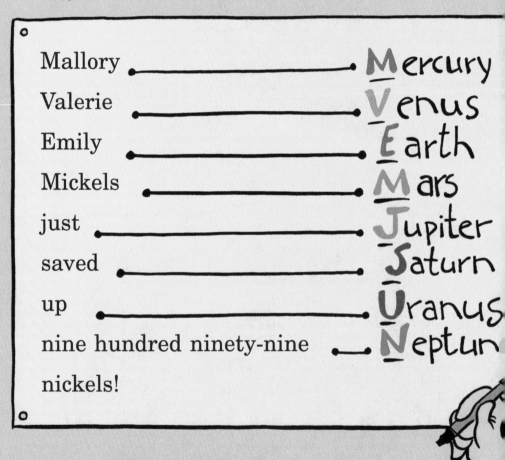

Mallory ———————— **M**ercury

Valerie ———————— **V**enus

Emily ———————— **E**arth

Mickels ———————— **M**ars

just ———————— **J**upiter

saved ———————— **S**aturn

up ———————— **U**ranus

nine hundred ninety-nine — **N**eptun

nickels!

The first letter of each
of these words is the same
as the first letter in each
of the planets you name.

Now here is a game
you can play in the skies:
Connect all the stars
you can see with your eyes.

GREAT DOG

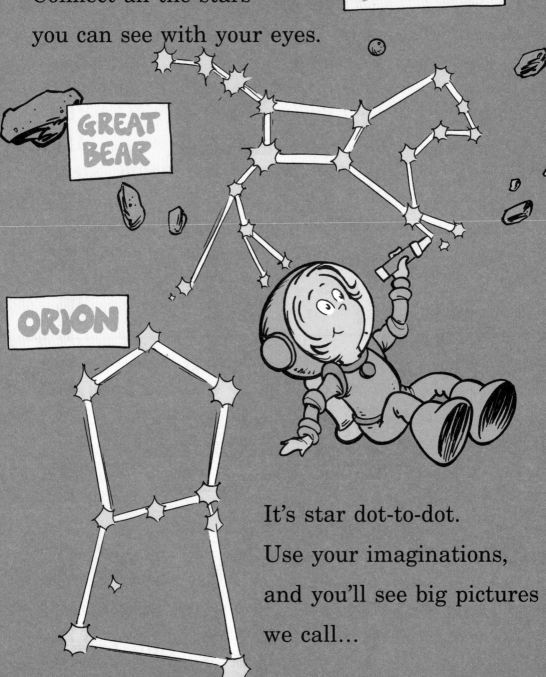
GREAT
BEAR

ORION

It's star dot-to-dot.
Use your imaginations,
and you'll see big pictures
we call...

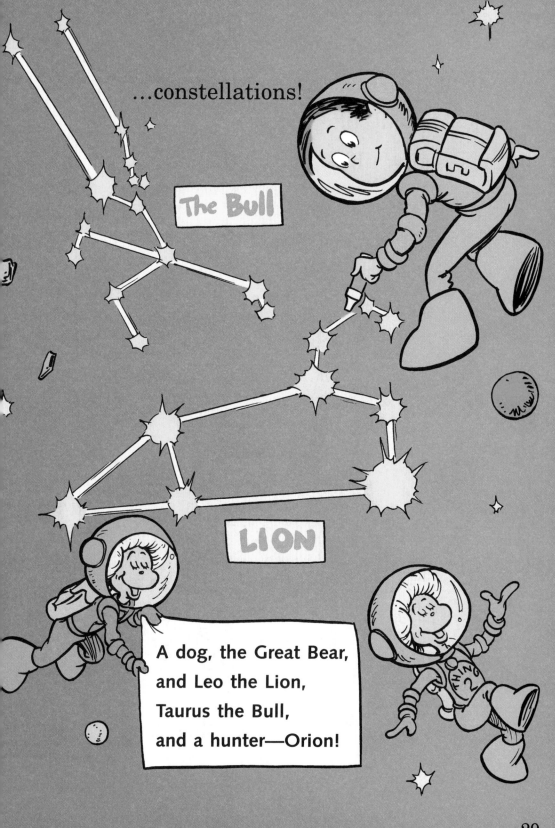

...constellations!

The Bull

LION

A dog, the Great Bear,
and Leo the Lion,
Taurus the Bull,
and a hunter—Orion!

A star in the sky
may look small, like a dot,
but it's really a big, glowing ball,
and it's **hot**.

And there's one star by far
that's our favorite one.
We can't live without it:
the star called…

...the sun!

From the Earth, it looks big.
There is one reason why.
It's the closest to Earth
of the stars in the sky.

But be careful and
never look right at the sun.
Your eyes would get hurt,
and that would not be fun.

How big is the sun?
We just heard
right this minute
a million of our Earths
could all fit right in it.

Oh, look at the time!
We must go very soon.
But first we must take
a quick look at the moon.

The moon does not shine
in the sky in the night
but, like a big mirror,
reflects the sun's light.

35

Astronauts flew
to the moon to explore
a place no one had
ever been to before!

They walked on the moon
and then drove all over
in a special moon car
called a lunar rover.

An astronomer studies what's up in the sky. Thing Two wants to be one. In fact, so do I!

The universe is
a mysterious place.
We are only just learning
what happens in space.

So I brought you a present!
To look in the sky—
just put this telescope
up to your eye.

Oh dear, I must go
fly back up to the stars
and take Things One and Two
out to dinner on Mars.

But there's lots to discover,
and it might be you
who looks up in the sky...

and finds something
that's new!

40

GLOSSARY

Astronaut: A person who pilots a spacecraft or works in space.

Astronomer: A person who studies the planets, stars, sun, moon, and other celestial bodies.

Constellation: A group of stars that form a pattern in the sky that looks like a picture.

Lunar rover: A vehicle used by astronauts to explore the surface of the moon.

Satellite: A natural or man-made object that moves around a planet.

Solar system: The sun and all the planets that move around it.

Telescope: An instrument that uses lenses to make faraway objects appear closer.

Universe: Everything that exists, including the earth, the planets, the stars, and all of space.

FOR FURTHER READING

The Big Dipper by Franklyn M. Branley, illustrated by Molly Coxe (HarperCollins, *Let's-Read-and-Find-Out Science®*, Stage 1). All about the Big Dipper, the Little Dipper, and the North Star. For preschoolers and up.

Is There Life in Outer Space? by Franklyn M. Branley, illustrated by Edward Miller (HarperCollins, *Let's-Read-and-Find-Out Science®*, Stage 1). A fun, informative introduction to the concept of life on other planets. For grades 1 and up.

Mars by Elizabeth Carney (National Geographic Kids, *National Geographic Readers*, Level 3). Illustrated with amazing photographs, this graded reader features information about Mars and our ongoing exploration of the planet. For grades 1 and up.

Moonwalk: The First Trip to the Moon by Judy Donnelly, illustrated by Dennis Davidson (Random House, *Step into Reading*, Step 5). The story of *Apollo II*'s historic flight, from liftoff to splashdown and quarantine. For grades 2 and up.

INDEX

astronauts, 36
astronomers, 37

constellations,
    28–29

Earth, 18–19, 33
    rotation of, 18–19

Great Bear, the, 29

Jupiter, 21

Leo, 29
lunar rover, 36

Mars, 20, 39
Mercury, 14
moon, 10, 34, 35,
    36

Neptune, 25

Orion, 29

planets, 8, 13, 21,
    24, 26, 27

satellites, 24
Saturn, 22–23
    rings of, 22
solar system, 13, 26
stars, 8, 10, 28, 30,
    31, 33, 39
sun, 8, 13, 14, 17,
    32–33, 35

Taurus, 29
telescope, 38

universe, 38
Uranus, 24

Venus, 16

The Cat in the Hat's Learning Library